HEY!

HEY, *ALEX!* HOLD ON!

ARE YOU *DOING* ANYTHING TONIGHT?

YEAH. *DOUBLE FRENCH AND HISTORY.* SORRY, SABINA.

ALEX, ARE YOU *OKAY?* I'VE HARDLY *SEEN* YOU ALL WEEK, AND YOU SEEM—

I'M *FINE.*

I'M *SORRY.* IT'S NOT BEING ABLE TO *TELL* ANYONE, YOU KNOW? HAVING ALL MY *FRIENDS* THINK I WAS OFF FOR TWO WEEKS WITH *FLU,* THAT I'M SOME *PAMPERED IDIOT...*

IT'S DRIVING ME *MAD.*

BORED, MORE LIKE.

YOU CAN'T WAIT FOR YOUR *SECRET AGENT BEEPER* TO GO OFF AGAIN, THAT'S YOUR TROUBLE.

I TOLD YOU, I'M **NOT** A SPY.

IT **WOULD** BE MORE EXCITING THAN **DOUBLE HOMEWORK**, THOUGH.

ANYWAY...

IT'S NOT **JUST** YOU WHO ISN'T ALLOWED TO TALK ABOUT IT, REMEMBER?

I HAD TO SIGN...

SABINA? WHAT IS IT?

THAT MAN IN THE **SKODA'S** HERE AGAIN.

THE **DRUG DEALER**.

YOU KNOW LUCY STILES WAS **BEATEN UP** THE OTHER DAY FOR HER **LUNCH MONEY**?

AND IT WENT STRAIGHT TO **SKODA**. SOMEBODY SHOULD **DO** SOMETHING ABOUT HIM.

YEAH.

THINGS HAVE BEEN **STOLEN**, TOO. HE'S **POISONING** THIS SCHOOL.

ANYWAY, I HAVE TO GO. I'LL SEE YOU **TOMORROW**, OKAY?

SURE. TAKE CARE!

HMMM...

WHAT'S HE *DOING* IN THERE?

HERE GOES NOTHING...

EW.

SOMEBODY SHOULD *DO* SOMETHING ABOUT HIM.

IT'S A FLOATING *DRUGS* FACTORY...!

MAYBE I SHOULD CALL THE *POLICE*.

...

OR BETTER YET...

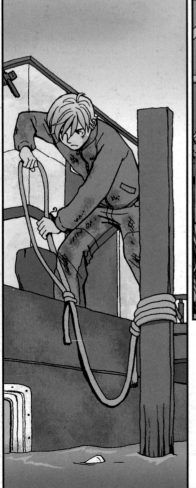

WOW.

WELL, *THIS* LOOKS EASY ENOUGH.

START

BEEP

WHIRRRR

SO I *SAID* TO 'IM, IF THAT'S *STRAIGHT* I'M A *DUTCHMAN*...

TOO RIGHT.

ZMMMMMM

POINT BLANC
ANTHONY HOROWITZ

Adapted by
Antony Johnston

Illustrated by
Kanako Damerum
& Yuzuru Takasaki

WALKER
BOOKS

First published 2007 by Walker Books Ltd
87 Vauxhall Walk, London SE11 5HJ

2 4 6 8 10 9 7 5 3 1

Text and illustrations © 2007 Walker Books Ltd
Based on the original novel *Point Blanc* © 2001 Anthony Horowitz

Anthony Horowitz has asserted his moral rights.

Trademarks 2007 Stormbreaker Productions Ltd
Alex Rider™, Boy with torch Logo™, AR Logo™

This book has been typeset in Lint McCree and Serpentine Bold
Printed in Italy

British Library Cataloguing in Publication Data:
a catalogue record for this book is available
from the British Library

ISBN 978-1-84428-112-1

www.walkerbooks.co.uk

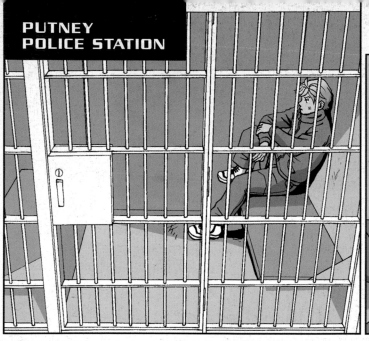

GOOD MORNING, ALEX.

MR CRAWFORD...

I *WONDERED* WHY NOBODY WOULD *TALK* TO ME AFTER THEY RAN MY NAME THROUGH THE *COMPUTER*.

YOU CAN COME WITH ME, NOW. WE'RE *LEAVING*.

WHERE *IS* EVERYONE? WHERE DID ALL THE *POLICEMEN* GO?

DON'T ASK *SILLY QUESTIONS*, ALEX. THIS WAY, PLEASE.

WHAT ABOUT MY *BIKE?* I LEFT IT BY THE BRIDGE...

DON'T WORRY, WE'VE *GOT* IT. AND YOUR *SCHOOLBOOKS*.

I HADN'T EXPECTED TO SEE YOU AGAIN SO **SOON**.

THAT'S JUST WHAT **I** WAS GOING TO SAY.

WHAT ON EARTH WERE YOU **THINKING?** YOU'VE DONE AN **ENORMOUS** AMOUNT OF DAMAGE. YOU PRACTICALLY **DESTROYED** A **TWO MILLION POUND** CONFERENCE CENTRE.

IT'S A MIRACLE NO ONE WAS **KILLED!**

THE MEN IN THE BOAT WILL BE IN **HOSPITAL** FOR **MONTHS**.

AND YOU COULD HAVE KILLED THE **HOME SECRETARY**, ALEX.

THEY'RE **DRUG DEALERS**.

SO WE'VE DISCOVERED. BUT THE **NORMAL** PROCEDURE IS TO CALL **999**.

I COULDN'T FIND A PHONE.

SIGH

WE WERE THINKING OF **CONTACTING** YOU, ANYWAY. WE **NEED** YOU AGAIN.

THIS IS *MICHAEL J. ROSCOE*, HEAD OF *ROSCOE ELECTRONICS*, ONE OF THE LARGEST COMPANIES IN *AMERICA*.

COMPUTERS, VIDEOS, DVD PLAYERS, MOBILE PHONES, WASHING MACHINES... ROSCOE WAS *VERY* RICH, *VERY* INFLUENTIAL—

AND *VERY* SHORT-SIGHTED, ACCORDING TO THE *NEWS*.

HE FELL DOWN A *LIFT SHAFT* A FEW WEEKS AGO, DIDN'T HE?

IT CERTAINLY *SEEMS* TO HAVE BEEN A CARELESS ACCIDENT. THE LIFT *MALFUNCTIONED*, ROSCOE DIDN'T *LOOK* WHERE HE WAS GOING, HE FELL INTO THE SHAFT AND *DIED*.

BUT WE'RE NOT SO *SURE*.

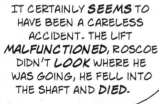

ON THE DAY ROSCOE DIED, AN *ENGINEER* CALLED AT *ROSCOE TOWER* TO CHECK A *DEFECTIVE CABLE*.

BUT THE COMPANY THAT *EMPLOYED* HIM SAY THERE *WAS* NO DEFECTIVE CABLE AND THEY NEVER *SENT* HIM TO THE TOWER.

SO WHY DON'T YOU ASK *HIM*?

OH, WE'D *LIKE* TO. BUT HE'S *VANISHED* WITHOUT TRACE. IT'S POSSIBLE HE WAS *KILLED*, AND SOMEONE ELSE TOOK HIS *PLACE* TO SET UP ROSCOE'S "ACCIDENT".

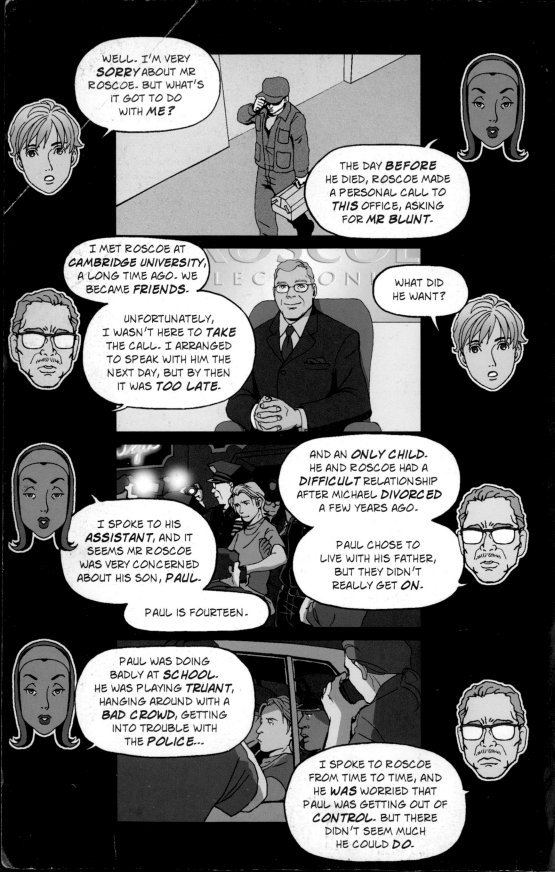

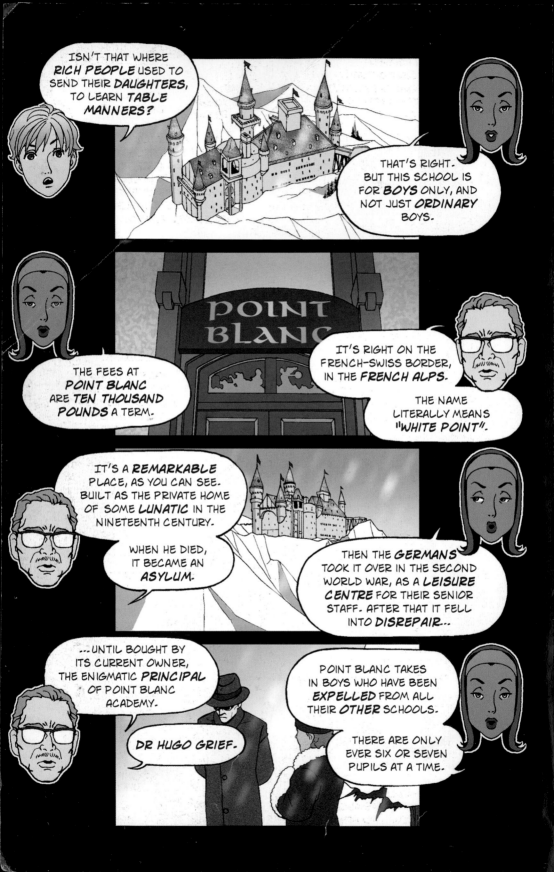

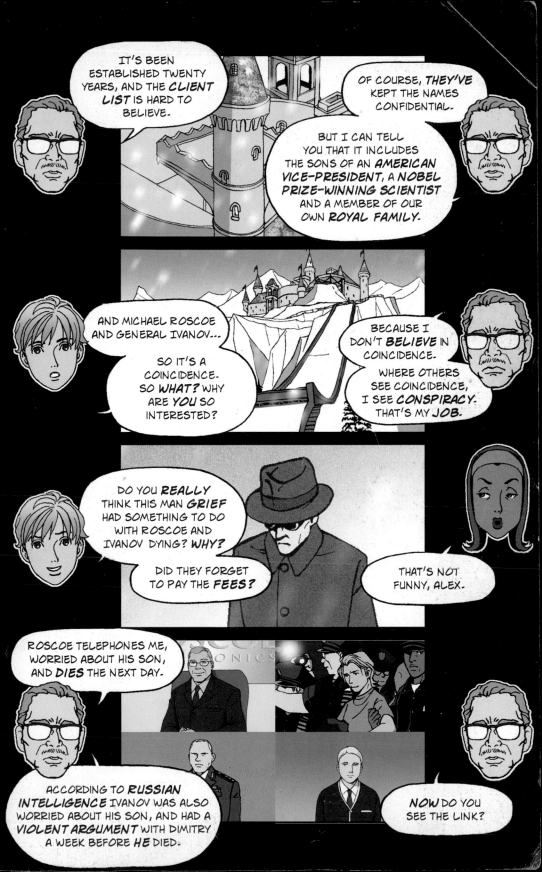

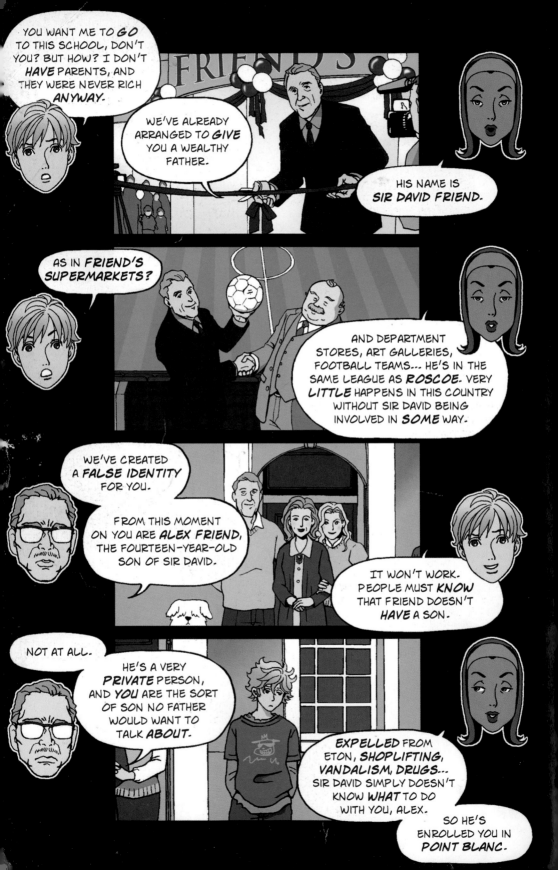

YOU HAVE **ONE WEEK** TO MEMORIZE YOUR **COVER STORY** AND THE FAMILY DETAILS. YOU'LL BE PICKED UP NEXT SATURDAY FROM THE FRIEND'S **COUNTRY ESTATE** IN **LANCASHIRE**.

AND WHAT DO I **DO** WHEN I GET TO THE SCHOOL?

SIMPLY FIND OUT **EVERYTHING** YOU CAN. IT **MAY** BE THAT POINT BLANC IS PERFECTLY **ORDINARY**, AND IN FACT THERE WAS **NO** CONNECTION BETWEEN THESE DEATHS.

IF SO, WE'LL PULL YOU OUT. WE JUST WANT TO BE **SURE**.

SORRY, ALEX.

THEY DON'T ALLOW **GAMES** IN THE SCHOOL. BUT WE'LL **ARRANGE** ALL THAT BEFORE YOU GO, DON'T WORRY.

...

HOW WILL I GET IN **TOUCH** WITH YOU? HAVE YOU MADE ME ANOTHER **NINTENDO**?

IN THE MEANTIME, WE'LL HAVE TO DO **SOMETHING** ABOUT YOUR **APPEARANCE**. YOU DON'T EXACTLY LOOK THE **PART**.

...WHAT?

POINT BLANC ACADEMY, FRANCE

I HADN'T **THOUGHT** OF THAT!

THE TROUBLE IS, I'M NOT REALLY A **FIELD AGENT**!

GET IT?

HAVE YOU GOT ME ANOTHER **NINTENDO?**

NO, THAT'S THE **PROBLEM**. THE ACADEMY DOESN'T **ALLOW** GAMES OF ANY SORT, OR EVEN **COMPUTERS**. THEY SUPPLY ALL THEIR **OWN**.

GROAN

ANYWAY, I'M **JOLLY** GLAD TO BE WORKING WITH YOU AGAIN. NOT OFTEN I GET A **TEENAGER**. MUCH MORE **FUN** THAN THE ADULTS!

MIND YOU, IT'S BEEN A BIT **TRICKY** THIS TIME...

NOW, I'M TOLD THERE'S A LOT OF **SNOW** UP ON POINT BLANC, SO YOU'LL NEED **THIS**. KNOW WHAT IT IS?

I'VE BEEN **SKIING** BEFORE, MR SMITHERS.

BUT NOT IN A SUIT LIKE **THIS**. IT'S HIGHLY **INSULATED**, AND ALSO **BULLET-PROOF**.

WOW.

THE DETONATION.

YOU SEE, IT'S A SMALL BUT POWERFUL **EXPLOSIVE**. **SEPARATING** THE PIECES AGAIN ACTIVATES THE **SECOND** STAGE,

A TEN-SECOND **COUNTDOWN**. THE BLAST WILL BLOW A HOLE IN ALMOST ANYTHING... OR **ANYONE**.

JUST SO LONG AS IT DOESN'T BLOW MY **EAR** OFF...

NO, NO, IT'S **PERFECTLY** SAFE WHILE YOU'RE **WEARING** IT. JUST DON'T TAKE IT **OUT** UNTIL YOU NEED TO **DESTROY** SOMETHING.

GOOD LUCK OLD CHAP!

GOODBYE, MR SMITHERS.

CHUGGA   CHUGGA...

COME BACK IN **ONE PIECE**. I REALLY DO **ENJOY** HAVING YOU AROUND!

CHUGGA   CHUGGA

WELL, IF THEY WANT A *NAUGHTY BOY*...

...THAT'S WHAT THEY'LL *GET*.

BRRRING

WHAT?

DINNER IS IN *TEN MINUTES*, ALEX. DON'T FORGET TO WEAR SMART CLOTHES!

HMMM.

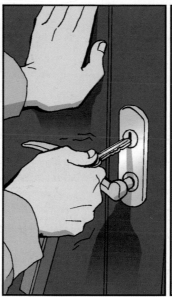

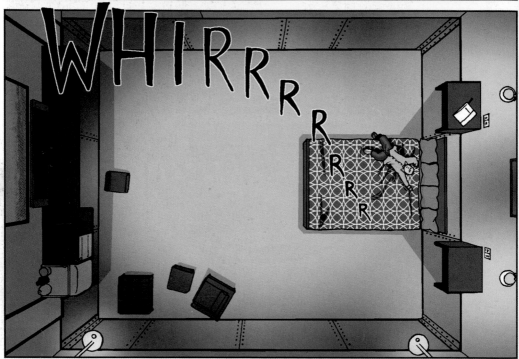

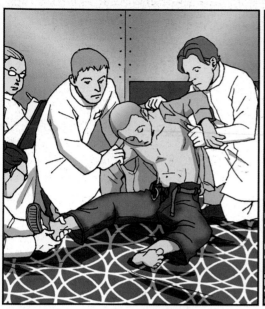

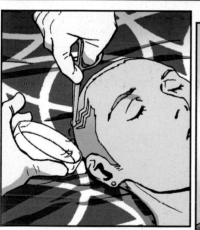

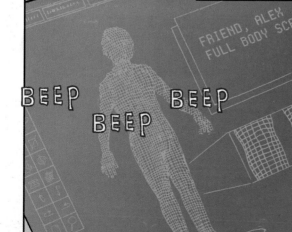

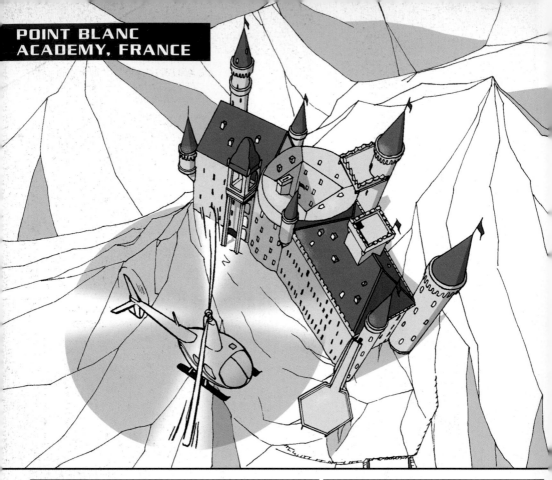

I'LL TAKE YOU DOWN TO MEET THE *DIRECTOR*. YOUR LUGGAGE WILL BE BROUGHT *FOR* YOU.

WE DON'T *USE* THE SKI JUMP, IT'S *FORBIDDEN*. COME DOWN, NOW, OUT OF THE *COLD*.

NICE PLACE.

YOU *THINK* SO? THE BUILDING WAS DESIGNED BY A *FRENCHMAN* WHO WAS CERTAINLY THE WORLD'S *WORST* ARCHITECT.

THIS WAS HIS *ONLY* COMMISSION. WHEN THE FIRST OWNERS MOVED IN, THEY HAD HIM *SHOT*.

THERE ARE STILL QUITE A *FEW* PEOPLE HERE WITH *GUNS*.

THAT'S VERY *KIND*, BUT I DON'T REALLY WANT TO *BE* HERE. SO IF YOU'LL JUST TELL ME HOW I CAN GET DOWN INTO *TOWN*, I'LL CATCH THE NEXT TRAIN HOME.

THERE IS *NO* WAY DOWN INTO TOWN. THE SKIING SEASON IS *OVER*, AND THE DESCENT IS NOW TOO *DANGEROUS*.

THERE IS ONLY THE *HELICOPTER*... AND THAT WILL TAKE YOU FROM HERE ONLY WHEN *I* SAY SO.

ALL THE BOYS HERE COME FROM FAMILIES OF GREAT *WEALTH* AND *IMPORTANCE*, LIKE YOURSELF.

WE COULD VERY EASILY BECOME A TARGET FOR *TERRORISTS*, SO THE GUARDS ARE FOR *YOUR* PROTECTION.

YOU ARE *HERE*, ALEX, BECAUSE YOU HAVE *DISAPPOINTED* YOUR PARENTS.

YOU WERE EXPELLED FROM SCHOOL, YOU HAVE HAD DIFFICULTIES WITH THE *POLICE*—

YOUR **ATTITUDE** IS AS DISPLEASING AS YOUR **APPEARANCE.** IT IS **OUR** JOB TO TURN YOU INTO A BOY OF WHOM YOUR PARENTS CAN BE **PROUD.**

I'M HAPPY AS I AM.

THAT WASN'T MY FAULT!

THAT IS OF **NO** RELEVANCE.

DON'T **INTERRUPT** THE DOCTOR!

FOR THE FIRST COUPLE OF WEEKS HERE,

YOU WILL **ASSIMILATE.**

I'LL **WHAT?**

ASSIMILATE. TO CONFORM... TO ADAPT... TO **BECOME LIKE.**

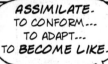

THERE ARE CURRENTLY **SIX** BOYS HERE.

YOU WILL MEET AND SPEND TIME WITH THEM, WITH OPPORTUNITIES FOR **SPORT, SOCIALIZING** AND **READING** IN OUR EXCELLENT LIBRARY. YOU WILL LEARN OUR **METHODS.**

I **HEARD** THAT!

I WANT TO CALL MY MUM AND DAD.

TELEPHONES ARE **FORBIDDEN.** SO ARE **PERSONAL COMPUTERS,** SO YOU CAN'T **E-MAIL** THEM EITHER. YOU MAY WRITE A **LETTER,** IF YOU LIKE.

UP YOURS.

YOU WILL BE **POLITE** TO THE ASSISTANT DIRECTOR!

YOU SHOULD **KNOW**, ALEX, THAT MRS STELLENBOSCH HAS WORKED WITH ME NOW FOR **TWENTY-SIX YEARS**.

WHEN I MET HER, SHE HAD BEEN **MISS SOUTH AFRICA** FIVE YEARS IN A ROW.

A **BEAUTY CONTEST**?

NO. **WEIGHTLIFTING**.

WE ENFORCE **STRICT DISCIPLINE** AT POINT BLANC.

BEDTIME IS TEN O'CLOCK **SHARP**. WE DO NOT TOLERATE **BAD LANGUAGE**. YOU WILL **NOT** CONTACT THE OUTSIDE WORLD WITHOUT OUR **PERMISSION**. YOU WILL **NOT** ATTEMPT TO LEAVE. YOU WILL DO AS YOU ARE TOLD **INSTANTLY**, WITHOUT HESITATION.

FINALLY, YOU ARE PERMITTED **ONLY** IN CERTAIN **PARTS** OF THE BUILDING.

YOU WILL REMAIN ON THE **GROUND** AND **FIRST** FLOORS **ONLY**, WHERE THE BEDROOMS AND CLASSROOMS ARE LOCATED.

THE SECOND AND THIRD FLOORS, **AND THE** BASEMENT, ARE **OUT OF BOUNDS**. THIS IS FOR YOUR **OWN** SAFETY.

GO NOW, AND WAIT **OUTSIDE**. SOMEONE WILL BE ALONG TO **COLLECT** YOU.

WE WILL MAKE YOU INTO WHAT YOUR PARENTS **WANT**, ALEX.

MAYBE THEY DON'T WANT ME AT **ALL**.

WE CAN ARRANGE **THAT** TOO.

DINING ROOM.

LIVING ROOM.

A COUPLE OF DAYS AGO I GOT INTO A *FIGHT* WITH TWO OF THEM, JUST FOR THE HELL OF IT. THEY BEAT THE *SNOT* OUT OF ME AND WENT *STRAIGHT* BACK TO THEIR *STUDIES!*

ANYWAY, I *GET* HERE AND IT'S LIKE A *MUSEUM* OR *MONASTERY* OR... I DON'T KNOW.

EVERYONE'S QUIET, HARD-WORKING, *BORING.* IT'S LIKE GRIEF SUCKED THEIR *BRAINS* OUT WITH A *STRAW.*

WEIRD.

YEAH.

DON'T TRY PLAYING *SNOOKER,* BY THE WAY. THE ROOM'S ON A *SLANT* AND ALL THE BALLS ROLL TO THE SIDE.

COME ON, THE *BEDROOMS* ARE UP HERE. I'LL SHOW YOU YOURS.

DO YOU HAVE THE *KEY?*

NO NEED. THE DOORS *CAN'T* BE *LOCKED.*

HERE YOU GO. THEY'VE PUT YOU NEXT TO ME.

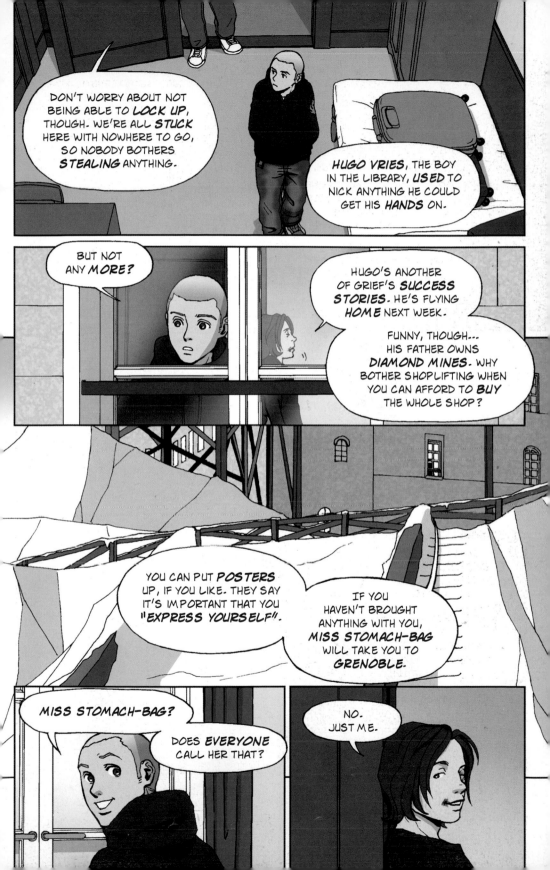

ALEX, THIS IS A DEEPLY *WEIRD* PLACE. I'VE BEEN TO A *LOT OF* SCHOOLS, BECAUSE I'VE BEEN *THROWN OUT* OF A LOT OF SCHOOLS... BUT THIS IS THE *PITS*.

THEY SAID THEY WANT US TO *ASSIMILATE*.

THAT'S *THEIR* WORD FOR IT, SURE. BUT THIS PLACE... THEY *CALL* IT A SCHOOL, BUT IT'S MORE LIKE BEING IN A *PRISON*. YOU SAW THE GUARDS?

I THOUGHT THEY WERE HERE TO *PROTECT* US.

I'VE BEEN HERE SIX WEEKS, AND HARDLY EVEN HAD ANY *LESSONS*. THEY HAVE *MUSIC* EVENINGS, AND *DISCUSSION* EVENINGS, AND THEY TRY TO GET ME TO *READ*, BUT OTHERWISE I'VE BEEN LEFT ON MY OWN.

THEN YOU'RE A BIGGER *IDIOT* THAN I THOUGHT.

THERE ARE ABOUT *THIRTY* OF THEM! FOR *SEVEN KIDS*!

THAT'S NOT PROTECTION, THAT'S *INTIMIDATION*.

SORRY, I SHOULDN'T LOSE MY *TEMPER*. IT'D JUST BE NICE TO THINK *SOMEONE'S* FINALLY ARRIVED THAT I CAN *RELATE* TO.

MAYBE YOU *CAN*.

YEAH, BUT FOR *HOW LONG?*

SEE YOU LATER, ALEX.

HMMM.

NO.
TOO SOON.

BRRRING   BRRRING

DINNER **ALREADY?**
TIME FLIES...

WHAT ON
EARTH...?

HUGO VRIES (14) Dutch, lives in Amsterdam. Father's name: Rudi, owns diamond mines. Speaks little English. Reads and plays guitar. Very solitary. Sent to PB for shoplifting and arson.

TOM McMORIN (14) Canadian, from Vancouver. Parents divorced. Mother runs media empire (newspapers, TV). Well-built, chess player. Car thefts and drunken driving.

NICOLAS MARC (14) French, from Bordeaux? Expelled from private school in Paris, cause unknown – drinking? Very fit all-rounder. Good at sport but hates losing. Tattoo of devil on left shoulder. Father: Anthony Marc – airlines, pop music, hotels. Never mentions his mother.

CASSIAN JAMES (14) American.
Mother: Jill, studio chief in
Hollywood. Parents divorced.
Loud voice. Swears a lot.
Plays jazz piano. Expelled from
three schools. Various drug
offences - sent to PB after
smuggling arrest but won't talk
about it now. One of the kids
who beat up James. Stronger
than he looks.

JOE CANTERBURY (14) American.
Spends a lot of time with Cassian
(helped him with James).
Mother (name unknown) New York
Senator. Father something big at
the Pentagon. Vandalism, truancy,
shoplifting. Sent to PB after
stealing and smashing up car.
Vegetarian. Permanently chewing
gum. Has he given up smoking?

JAMES SPRINTZ (14) German,
lives in Düsseldorf. Father: Dieter
Sprintz, banker, well-known
financier (the One Hundred Million
Dollar Man). Mother living in
England. Expelled for wounding a
teacher with an air pistol. My only
friend at PB! And the only one
who really hates it here.

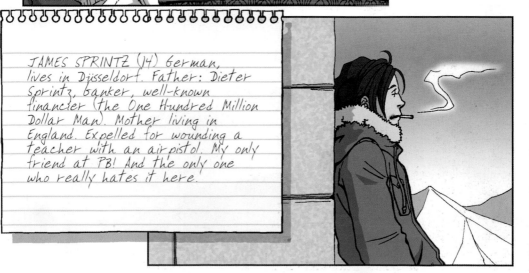

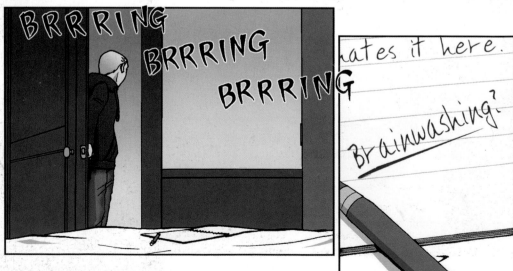

WILL YOU BE JOINING US FOR *LATIN* AFTER LUNCH, ALEX?

GET LOST.

WHAT'S THE MATTER, LATIN TOO *ADVANCED* FOR YOU? PERHAPS YOU'D PREFER YOUR *TIMES TABLES*, THAT SHOULD BE *EASY* ENOUGH!

HA HA HA!

I THOUGHT YOU WERE SUPPOSED TO BE A *HARD REBEL*, CASSIAN. BUT *LOOK* AT YOU, SUCKING UP TO A *PATHETIC OLD MAN!*

DON'T YOU *TALK* ABOUT THE DOCTOR LIKE THAT! HE'S A *GENIUS!*

COME ON, LET'S GO AND GET SOME *FRESH AIR*. I FEEL *SICK*.

THIS WAY.

ALEX! ARE YOU *COMING*?

IT'S GONE...

WHAT'S GONE?

...I DON'T *KNOW*. NOTHING.

MY EYES MUST BE PLAYING *TRICKS* ON ME.

WHAT THE...?

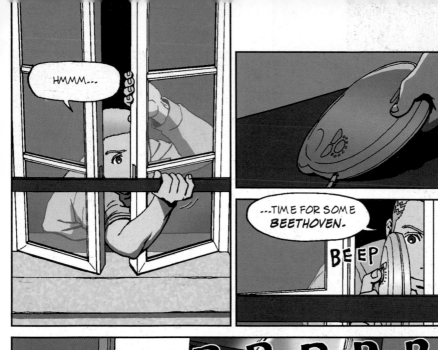

SLAM!

KOF! KOF!

DAMN.

KLANG
KLANG

METAL?
THAT'S WEIRD.

LIBRARY

OH!

EVEN THE **BOOKS** ARE THE SAME...

LIBRARY

IS IT **ALL** LIKE THIS?

WAIT, **THIS** IS NEW.

IT CAN'T BE **THIS** LIBRARY, BECAUSE **I'M** NOT IN THE PICTURE... IT MUST BE THE ONE **DOWNSTAIRS.**

SO YOU CAN SIT IN ONE AND **WATCH** THE OTHER.

BUT **WHY?** WHAT'S THE **POINT?**

I ALWAYS **WAS** THE BEST. BUT THAT'S WHAT YOU **PAID** FOR.

AND WHILE WE'RE **ON** THAT SUBJECT, MAYBE WE SHOULD TALK ABOUT MY FINAL **PAYMENT?**

FOR MY **WORK,** YES. MY **SILENCE** IS ANOTHER MATTER.

I WAS THINKING ANOTHER **QUARTER MILLION.** GIVEN THE SIZE OF YOUR **GEMINI PROJECT,** IT'S NOT SO MUCH TO ASK.

THEN I'LL RETIRE TO **SPAIN** AND YOU'LL NEVER HEAR FROM ME AGAIN, I **PROMISE.**

YOU HAVE **ALREADY** BEEN PAID **ONE MILLION** AMERICAN DOLLARS, MR BAXTER.

OF **COURSE,** DR GRIEF. BUT I THOUGHT YOU MIGHT LIKE TO CONSIDER A LITTLE ... **BONUS.**

WE HAD AN **AGREEMENT.**

I WILL **NEVER** HEAR FROM YOU **AGAIN...** YES.

YES, I THINK THAT IS A **GOOD IDEA.**

PTUI!

THIS IS *GRIEF*.

I HAVE SOME *GARBAGE* IN THE OPERATING THEATRE THAT NEEDS TO BE REMOVED. INFORM THE *DISPOSAL TEAM*.

SHHHHHUNK

SHHHHHHUNK

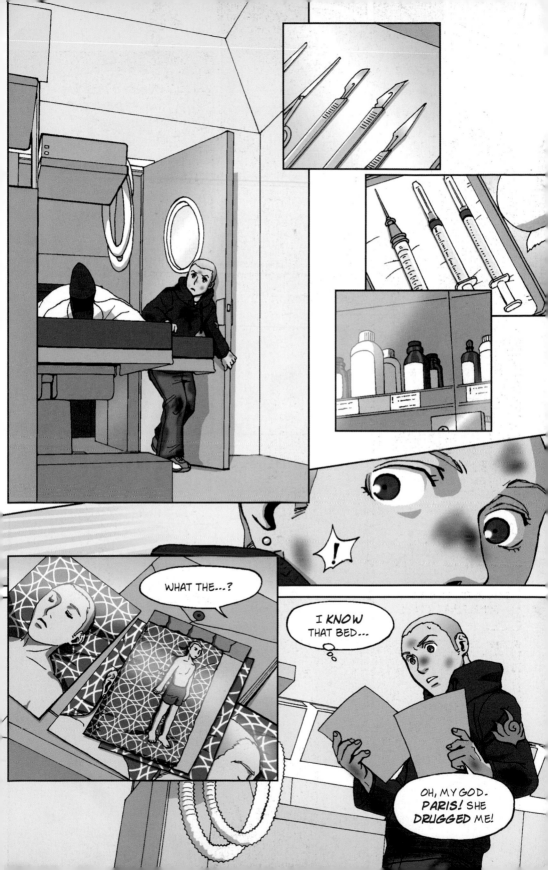

WE'VE HEARD FROM *ALEX*.

HE SENT THE *PANIC SIGNAL* FROM HIS PORTABLE SATELLITE TRANSMITTER THIS MORNING, AT *1027 HOURS* HIS TIME.

MOST URGENT

WE HAVE TO PULL HIM *OUT*.

I *WONDER*. ALEX HAS BEEN AT POINT BLANC FOR JUST *ONE WEEK*, YES? AND WE KNOW HE DIDN'T WANT TO GO IN THE *FIRST* PLACE.

HE *SENT* THE SIGNAL, ALAN!

THAT MEANS HE'S EITHER *FOUND* SOMETHING OR HE'S IN *DANGER*. EITHER WAY, WE CAN'T JUST SIT BACK AND DO *NOTHING!*

ALEX MAY NO LONGER BE *100%* RELIABLE.

I WASN'T *SUGGESTING* THAT.

YOU SEEM TO BE FORMING QUITE AN *ATTACHMENT* TO ALEX, MRS JONES. YOU HAVE CHILDREN OF YOUR *OWN*, DON'T YOU?

THAT'S NOT THE POINT. ALEX IS *SPECIAL*.

WE CAN'T GO *BLUNDERING* INTO POINT BLANC WITHOUT *FIRM* INFORMATION.

THIS IS *FRANCE* WE'RE TALKING ABOUT. IF WE'RE SEEN TO BE INVADING THEIR *TERRITORY* THEY'LL KICK UP ONE *HELL* OF A FUSS.

BESIDES, GRIEF HAS BOYS FROM SOME OF THE *WEALTHIEST* FAMILIES IN THE *WORLD.* WE GO *STORMING IN* AND THE WHOLE THING COULD BLOW UP INTO A *MAJOR INTERNATIONAL INCIDENT.*

ALEX MAY HAVE THE *PROOF* YOU NEED TO *CONNECT* GRIEF WITH THE DEATHS OF *ROSCOE* AND *IVANOV.*

AND HE MAY *NOT.*

...

A *TWENTY-FOUR HOUR DELAY* SHOULDN'T MAKE MUCH DIFFERENCE. WE'LL PUT AN *SAS UNIT* ON STANDBY. IF ALEX *IS* IN TROUBLE, WE'LL FIND OUT SOON ENOUGH.

AND IF ALEX CONTACTS US *AGAIN?*

THEN WE'LL GO IN.

AND IT COULD PLAY TO OUR *FAVOUR* IF HE'S MANAGED TO STIR THINGS *UP.* FORCE GRIEF TO SHOW HIS *HAND.*

ASSUMING HE'S NOT ALREADY *DEAD.*

SLAM!

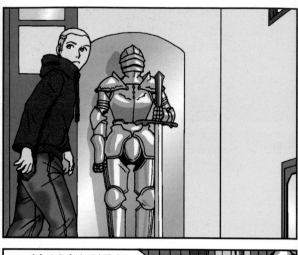

COME ON, THERE *MUST* BE A WAY TO OPEN IT FROM *THIS* SIDE, TOO...

HMMM. A *RAISED* BUTTON...

KLIK!

WOAH.

WHRRRRRR

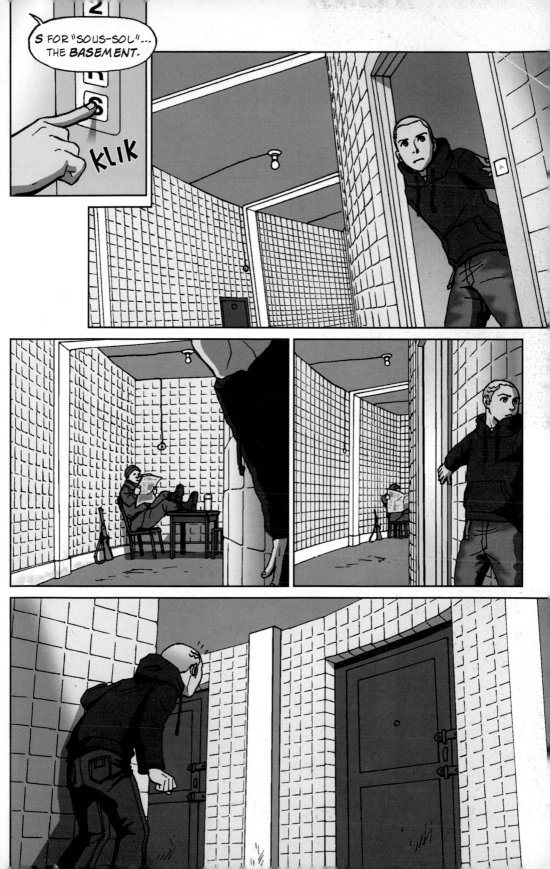

MMMMMMM

COME ON, COME ON...

ALEX! WHAT ARE YOU *DOING* HERE?

SHHH, KEEP YOUR VOICE *DOWN!* WE HAVEN'T GOT MUCH TIME... WHAT *HAPPENED* TO YOU?

THEY CAME THE NIGHT BEFORE *LAST.* DRAGGED ME OUT OF *BED* AND INTO THE *LIBRARY.* THERE'S A *LIFT—*

BEHIND THE *ARMOUR,* I KNOW. WHAT DID THEY SAY?

NOTHING. NO ONE WOULD *TELL* ME WHAT WAS GOING ON, THEY JUST THREW ME IN *HERE!*

YOU'VE BEEN HERE FOR *TWO DAYS?* BUT I JUST SAW YOU *UPSTAIRS,* HAVING *BREAKFAST!*

THEY'VE MADE *DUPLICATES* OF US, DUDE.

ALL OF US. I DON'T KNOW *HOW* OR *WHY,* BUT THAT'S WHAT'S GOING *DOWN.* I'VE BEEN HERE FOR *MONTHS.*

I'M PAUL, BY THE WAY. *PAUL ROSCOE.*

ROSCOE? ARE YOU *MICHAEL* ROSCOE'S SON?

YEAH, WHY?

...NOTHING.

HOW DID YOU GET *DOWN* HERE, ALEX? WHAT'S GOING *ON*?

ALL RIGHT, LISTEN CAREFULLY.

MY NAME *ISN'T* ALEX FRIEND, IT'S *ALEX RIDER*. I WAS SENT HERE BY *MI6*. AND EVERYTHING'S GOING TO BE OK. THEY'RE SENDING PEOPLE IN TO *FREE* YOU ALL.

YOU'RE... A *SPY*?

SORT OF. I SUPPOSE.

DUDE, WHAT ARE WE *WAITING* FOR? LET'S GET *OUTTA* HERE!

NO!

YOU'VE GOT TO *WAIT*. THERE'S NO WAY DOWN THE *MOUNTAIN*.

STAY HERE FOR NOW AND I'LL COME BACK WITH HELP, I *PROMISE*. IT'S THE *ONLY* WAY.

I'LL COME *BACK*, I—

—PROMISE.

BUT I *CAN'T*—

YOU *HAVE TO*. *TRUST* ME, PAUL. I'M GOING TO LOCK YOU BACK IN, SO NOBODY WILL KNOW I'VE *BEEN* HERE. BUT IT WON'T BE FOR *LONG*.

UNH!

"HIRED"?

HAAAAHAHAHA!

HAH

YOU HAVE **NO IDEA** WHAT YOU'VE SEEN, DO YOU?

YOUR LITTLE MIND CANNOT **BEGIN** TO ENCOMPASS WHAT **I** HAVE ACHIEVED!

LISTEN **CAREFULLY,** ALEX, AND I SHALL DESCRIBE TO YOU THE **GEMINI PROJECT.**

WHEN YOU GO SCREAMING TO YOUR **DEATH,** YOU WILL UNDERSTAND THAT YOU COULD **NEVER** HOPE TO BEAT A MAN SUCH AS **I.** PERHAPS THAT WILL MAKE DYING **EASIER** FOR YOU.

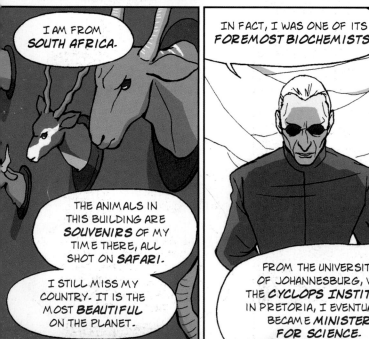

I AM FROM **SOUTH AFRICA.**

THE ANIMALS IN THIS BUILDING ARE **SOUVENIRS** OF MY TIME THERE, ALL SHOT ON **SAFARI.**

I STILL MISS MY COUNTRY. IT IS THE MOST **BEAUTIFUL** ON THE PLANET.

IN FACT, I WAS ONE OF ITS **FOREMOST BIOCHEMISTS.**

FROM THE UNIVERSITY OF JOHANNESBURG, VIA THE **CYCLOPS INSTITUTE** IN PRETORIA, I EVENTUALLY BECAME **MINISTER FOR SCIENCE.**

WHEN YOU SAID WERE GOING TO **KILL** ME, I DIDN'T REALISE YOU MEANT BY **BORING** ME TO DEATH.

UNH!

ENOUGH.

LET HIM *HAVE* HIS LITTLE JOKE. THERE WILL BE PLENTY OF *PAIN* FOR HIM *LATER.*

ONCE, ALEX, THE *WHITE PEOPLE* OF SOUTH AFRICA RULED *EVERYTHING.*

UNDER THE LAWS THE REST OF THE WORLD CALLED *APARTHEID*, BLACK PEOPLE COULD NOT *LIVE NEAR* WHITE PEOPLE. THEY COULD NOT *MARRY* WHITE PEOPLE. THEY HAD SEPARATE *TOILETS, RESTAURANTS, BARS...* THEY HAD TO CARRY *PASSES*, AND WERE TREATED LIKE *ANIMALS.*

YEAH. IT WAS *DISGUSTING.*

NO!

IT WAS *PERFECT!*

BUT AS TIME PASSED, I SAW IT WOULD BE *SHORT-LIVED.*

THE REST OF THE WORLD WAS *GANGING UP* ON US. I FORESAW THE DAY THAT A *CRIMINAL* LIKE *NELSON MANDELA* COULD TAKE POWER!

HOW **WEAK** AND **PATHETIC** THE WORLD WAS BECOMING... **DETERMINED** TO GIVE AWAY A **GREAT** COUNTRY LIKE MINE TO PEOPLE WHO HAD **NO IDEA** HOW TO RUN IT.

OH, GREAT. ANOTHER **WANNABE WORLD CONQUEROR.**

OOF!

I LOOKED **AROUND** AND SAW THAT THE PEOPLE OF AMERICA AND EUROPE HAD BECOME **STUPID** AND **WEAK.** THE FALL OF THE **BERLIN WALL** ONLY MADE THINGS WORSE. SOON, EVEN **RUSSIA** WAS INFECTED WITH THE SAME DISEASE.

AND I THOUGHT TO MYSELF, HOW MUCH **STRONGER** THE WORLD WOULD BE IF **I** RULED IT. HOW MUCH **BETTER.**

ON THE **CONTRARY,** IT HAS BEEN THE AMBITION OF VERY **FEW** MEN TO RULE THE ENTIRE WORLD. HITLER, NAPOLEON, STALIN... GREAT MEN, **REMARKABLE** MEN!

MEN LIKE **ME!**

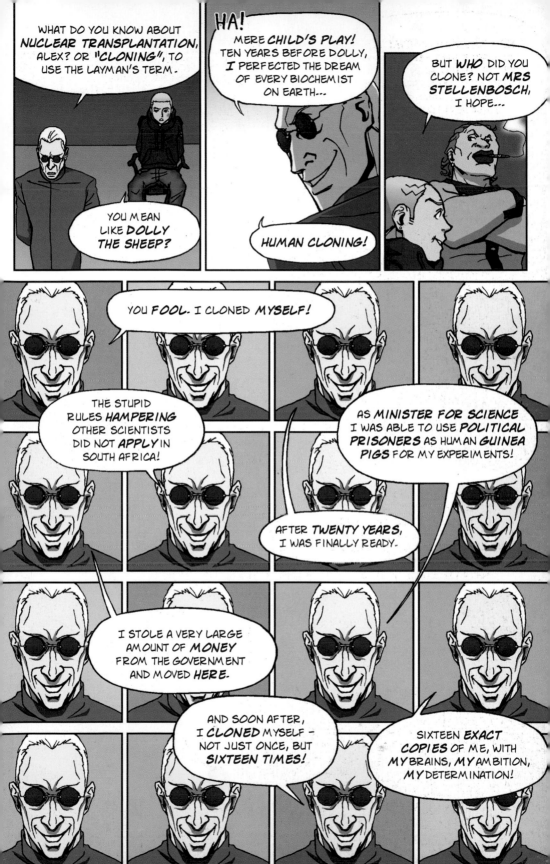

ROSCOE DID NOT BELIEVE WHAT HE SAW. NEITHER DID THAT IDIOT RUSSIAN, *GENERAL IVANOV*. THEY DID NOT GUESS WHAT *REALLY* HAPPENED, BUT THEY KNEW *SOMETHING* WAS WRONG.

BUT *ROSCOE* NOTICED, DIDN'T HE? THAT'S WHY YOU HAD HIM *KILLED*.

STILL, TWO OUT OF SIXTEEN IS *NOT* SUCH A CATASTROPHE.

GEMINI HAS BEEN AN *OUTSTANDING* SUCCESS. THE LAST OF THE CHILDREN WILL *RETURN* TO THEIR FAMILIES IN A FEW DAY'S TIME.

OF COURSE, I MUST *DISPOSE* OF THE *ORIGINALS*. THEY WILL DIE *PAINLESSLY*.

BUT NOT *YOU*, ALEX RIDER.

TOMORROW'S FIRST LESSON IS *DOUBLE BIOLOGY*. MY CHILDREN RECENTLY ASKED TO SE A *HUMAN DISSECTION*. TOMORROW, I WILL *GRANT* THEIR WISH.

THROW HIM IN ONE OF THE *HIGH SECURITY* CELLS!

WE SHALL *NOT* USE *ANAESTHETIC*. I EXPECT IT WILL BE *VERY PAINFUL* FOR YOU.

TAKE HIS **BELT**, **SHOELACES** AND EVERYTHING IN HIS **POCKETS**. HERR GRIEF SUSPECTS THE BOY MAY ATTEMPT **SUICIDE**.

YEAH, RIGHT. NOT UNLESS I COULD TAKE HIM **WITH** ME.

THIS IS ALL **POINTLESS**, YOU KNOW! **MIG** WILL BE HERE **ANY MINUTE!**

SLAM!

1100 HOURS

ANY MINUTE...

1300 HOURS

1500 HOURS

1700 HOURS

2000 HOURS

2300 HOURS

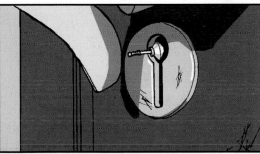

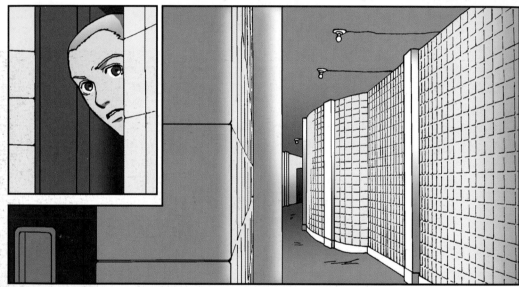

HE'S *IMPROVISED* SOME KIND OF *SLEIGH* OR *TOBOGGAN*. PERHAPS HE'S NOT SUCH AN *IDIOT* AFTER ALL.

I WANT TWO MEN ON *SNOWMOBILES* TO FOLLOW HIM DOWN. *NOW!*

WHAT ABOUT THE UNIT AT THE *FOOT* OF THE *MOUNTAIN?* WHATEVER HE'S USING, HE'LL BE UNABLE TO CROSS THE *RAILWAY LINE* INTO THE *LA VALLÉE DE FER.*

TRUE. VERY WELL, HAVE OUR MEN IN THE VAN READY THE *MACHINE GUN.*

ALEX RIDER WILL BE A *SITTING DUCK.*

AND I WILL SEE BOTH OF *YOU* IN MY OFFICE TOMORROW MORNING.

I WOULD HAVE LIKED TO *WATCH* HIM DIE, BUT NEVER MIND. LET US RETURN TO *BED.*

HIER KOMMT DER JUNGE.

WARTE... NICHT SCHIESSEN BIS ER NÄHER IST!

W SSS SS H

LA VALLÉE DE FER...

...AND THERE ARE THE TRAIN TRACKS JAMES MENTIONED.

FEUER!

BRAKKA

BRAKKA

BRAKKA

WHUMP

WOOO-HOO!

HA HA!

SO LONG—

KRRRRCH!

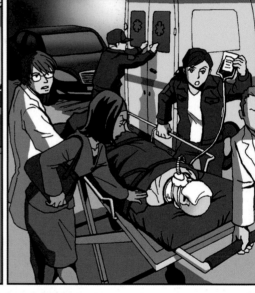

FRAU STELLENBOSCH? ICH HABE *GUTE* NACHRICHTEN FÜR SIE...

I AM EVA STELLENBOSCH, ASSISTANT DIRECTOR OF POINT BLANC ACADEMY.

I UNDERSTAND ONE OF OUR STUDENTS, ALEX FRIEND, WAS BROUGHT HERE THIS MORNING.

AH, YES. TAKE A SEAT, MRS STELLENBOSCH. THE DOCTOR WILL BE OUT IN A MOMENT.

SNIFF

MADAME STELLENBOSCH?

PLEASE REMAIN SEATED, MADAME.

YOU MUST UNDERSTAND, ALEX TRIED TO SNOWBOARD DOWN THE MOUNTAIN AT NIGHT. HE COLLIDED WITH A TRAIN AT HIGH SPEED...

HE BROKE BOTH ARMS, HIS COLLARBONE AND ONE OF HIS LEGS. HIS SKULL WAS FRACTURED. WE OPERATED AS SOON AS WE COULD, BUT THERE WAS MASSIVE INTERNAL BLEEDING AND HE WENT INTO SHOCK.

I'M SORRY, MADAME. ALEX FRIEND IS DEAD.

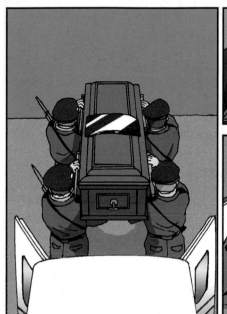

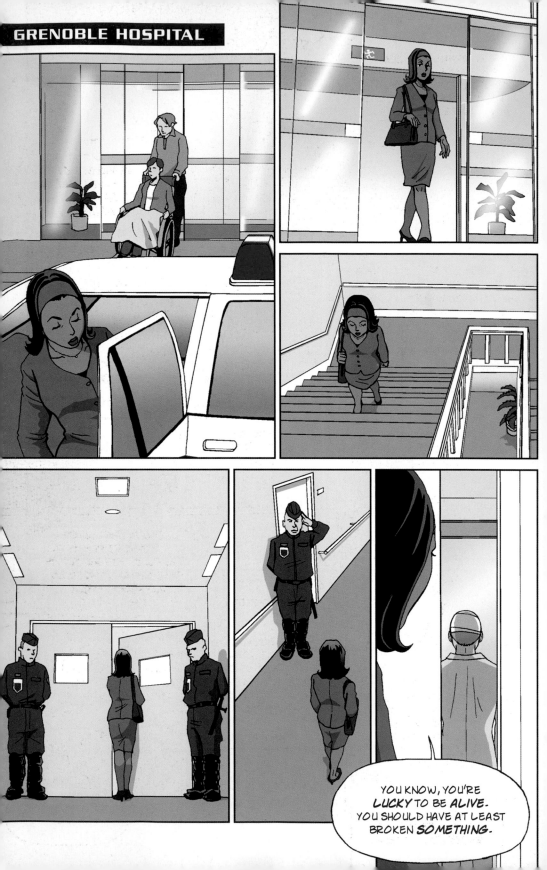

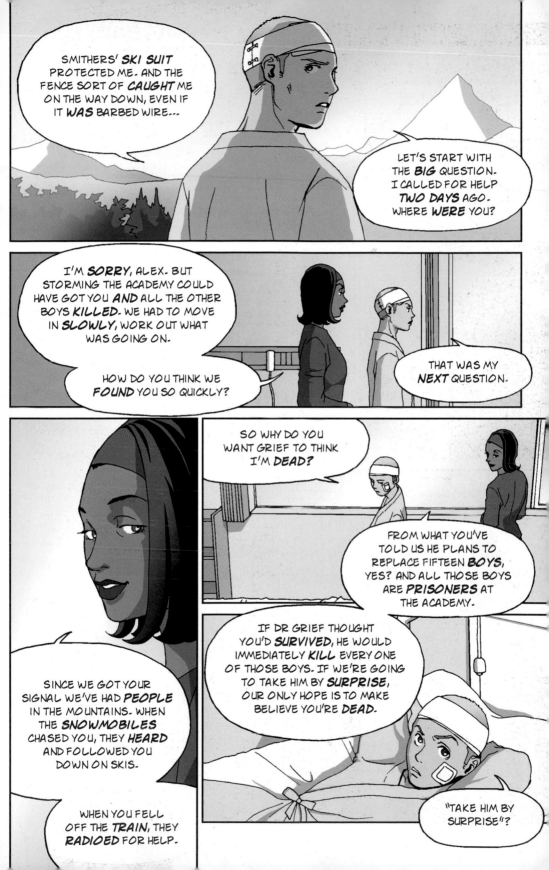

WOLF! WHAT ARE *YOU* DOING HERE?

THEY CALLED ME IN TO *CLEAR UP* THE MESS *YOU* LEFT BEHIND.

SORRY I DIDN'T BRING YOU *FLOWERS* AND *GRAPES*.

ALEX HAS DONE A *VERY* GOOD JOB SO FAR. BUT THERE ARE STILL *FIFTEEN* YOUNG *PRISONERS* AT POINT BLANC, AND OUR PRIORITY IS TO *SAVE* THEM.

SO WHERE WERE *YOU* WHEN I WAS BEING CHASED DOWN THE MOUNTAIN BY *HOMICIDAL SNOWMOBILE RIDERS?*

YOU SEEMED TO BE DOING FINE ON YOUR *OWN*.

ALEX SAYS THERE ARE ABOUT *THIRTY* GUARDS IN AND AROUND THE SCHOOL.

THE *ONLY* CHANCE THOSE BOYS HAVE IS FOR AN *SAS UNIT* TO BREAK IN.

AND THAT UNIT WILL BE COMMANDED BY *WOLF*.

WHERE DOES THE *BOY* COME INTO THIS?

ALEX *KNOWS* THE SCHOOL, THE POSITION OF THE GUARDS AND THE LOCATION OF THE *PRISON CELLS*. HE CAN LEAD YOU TO THE LIFT—

NO.

HE CAN TELL US *EVERYTHING* WE NEED TO KNOW RIGHT *HERE* AND *NOW*.

TWO KILOMETRES
NORTH OF POINT BLANC

UNH!

WHERE'S THIS *LIFT?*

THE *LIBRARY.* FOLLOW ME.

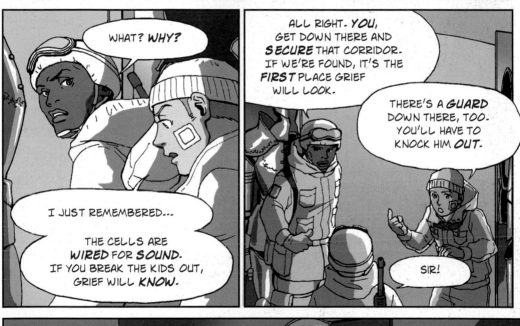

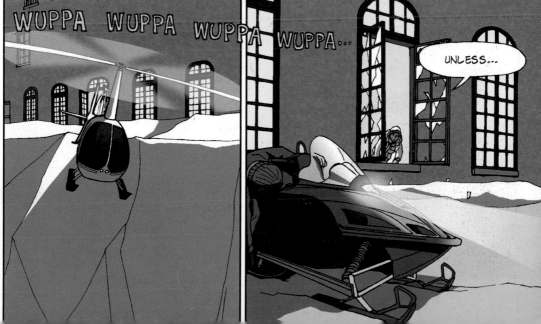

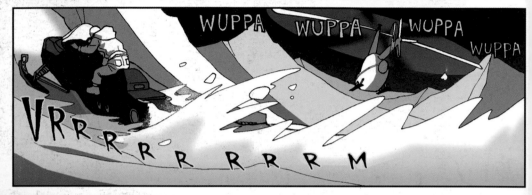

IT SEEMS WE OWE YOU A DEBT OF *THANKS*.

YOU DON'T OWE ME *ANYTHING*.

LIVERPOOL STREET
TWO DAYS LATER

RUBBISH. YOU HAVE CHANGED THE VERY *FUTURE* OF THIS PLANET. GRIEF'S... *OFFSPRING*... COULD HAVE CAUSED *MANY* PROBLEMS.

BUT WE HAVE ALL FIFTEEN OF THEM UNDER *LOCK AND KEY*, NOW. THEY WERE *TRACED* AND *ARRESTED* BY THE INTELLIGENCE SERVICES OF EACH COUNTRY WHERE THEY *LIVED*.

OF COURSE, WE'VE HUSHED IT *UP*. CLONING *SHEEP* IS ONE THING, BUT *HUMAN BEINGS*...!

THE FAMILIES DON'T WANT *PUBLICITY*, THEY'RE JUST GLAD TO HAVE THEIR SONS *BACK*. AND YOU'VE ALREADY SIGNED THE *OFFICIAL SECRETS ACT*, SO I'M SURE WE CAN TRUST *YOU* TO BE DISCREET.

HOW'S *WOLF*?

STILL IN *HOSPITAL*, BUT THE DOCTORS SAY HE'LL MAKE A *COMPLETE* RECOVERY IN A FEW *WEEKS*.

WE HAD *ONE* FATALITY, THE MAN YOU SAW SHOT BY DR GRIEF. WOLF AND ANOTHER MAN WERE *INJURED*. OTHERWISE, IT WAS A *COMPLETE SUCCESS*.

YOU *LEFT* ME THERE. I CALLED FOR HELP AND YOU *DIDN'T COME*. GRIEF WAS GOING TO *KILL* ME, BUT *YOU DIDN'T CARE*.

I USED TO THINK BEING A SPY WOULD BE *EXCITING* AND *SPECIAL*. BUT YOU JUST *USED* ME. IN A WAY, YOU'RE AS BAD AS *GRIEF*. YOU'LL DO *ANYTHING* TO GET WHAT YOU WANT.

IT DOESN'T MATTER. I'VE HAD *ENOUGH*. I DON'T WANT TO BE A *SPY* ANY MORE. IF YOU ASK ME AGAIN, I'LL *REFUSE*.

THAT'S NOT *TRUE!* THERE WERE *DIFFICULTIES...*

I KNOW YOU THINK YOU CAN *BLACKMAIL* ME, BUT THAT WON'T WORK ANY MORE. I *KNOW* TOO MUCH.

WELL, *I* WANT TO GO BACK TO SCHOOL. NEXT TIME, YOU CAN DO IT *WITHOUT* ME.

HE'LL BE BACK.

YOU REALLY *THINK* SO?

HE'S TOO *GOOD* AT THE JOB. IT'S IN HIS *BLOOD*.

MOST SCHOOLBOYS *DREAM* OF BEING A SPY. ALEX IS A SPY WHO DREAMS OF BEING A *SCHOOLBOY*.

JACK? I'M BACK... WHAT'S FOR LUNCH?

OH, ALEX! I THOUGHT YOU'D ONLY JUST GONE *OUT* AGAIN.

THE *SCHOOL* CALLED A FEW MINUTES AGO. SOMEONE CALLED *MR BRAY* WANTS TO SEE YOU AT THREE O'CLOCK.

BRAY'S THE *HEADMASTER.*

HE PROBABLY WANTS TO SEE ME ABOUT MY *ABSENCES* AGAIN.

NO, I'LL HAVE SOMETHING WHEN I GET *BACK.* SEE YOU LATER!

IT'S *TWENTY TO THREE* NOW. I'D BETTER GET *GOING.*

WHAT ABOUT YOUR *LUNCH?* SHALL I MAKE YOU A SANDWICH?

BROOKLAND SCHOOL

YOU AGAIN!

HELLO, BERNIE.

ON YOUR WAY TO SEE *MR BRAY*?

YEAH.

HE NEVER TOLD *ME* HE WAS GOING TO BE HERE TODAY.

BUT THEN, HE NEVER TELLS ME *ANYTHING!*

I'LL BE BACK AT *FIVE* TO LOCK UP. MAKE SURE YOU'RE OUT BY THEN.

OK. SEE YOU, BERNIE!

SCIENCE
BLOCK

Mr. Bray
Headmaster

KNOCK KNOCK

COME IN!

YOU WANTED
TO *SEE* ME?

ANTHONY HOROWITZ (BA/Neilsen Author of the Year 2007) is one of the most popular children's writers working today. His hugely successful Alex Rider series has sold over ten million copies worldwide and won numerous awards, including the Children's Book of the Year Award for ARK ANGEL at the 2006 British Book Awards and the Red House Children's Book Award for SKELETON KEY. He scripted the blockbuster movie STORMBREAKER from his own novel, and also writes extensively for TV, with programmes including MIDSOMER MURDERS, POIROT and FOYLE'S WAR. He is married to television producer Jill Green and lives in London with his two sons, Nicholas and Cassian, and their dog, Loser.

www.anthonyhorowitz.com

ANTONY JOHNSTON, who wrote the script for this book, has written more than a dozen other graphic novels, including THE LONG HAUL, JULIUS, and ROSEMARY'S BACKPACK, and two monthly comics series, WASTELAND and TEXAS STRANGERS. He's also penned several miniseries, and more short stories than he can remember. In addition to his comics work, he writes novels, such as FRIGHTENING CURVES (which won the 2002 IPPY award for Best Horror) and STEALING LIFE. Antony lives in north-west England with the loves of his life: his partner Marcia, his dogs Connor and Rosie, and his iMac. The iMac doesn't have a name.

www.antonyjohnston.com

The artwork in this graphic novel is the work of two artists, **KANAKO DAMERUM** and **YUZURU TAKASAKI,** who collaborate on every illustration. Although living on opposite sides of the globe, these Japanese sisters work seamlessly together via the Internet.

Living and working in Tokyo, **YUZURU** produced all the line work for these illustrations using traditional means. The quality of her draughtsmanship comes from years of honing her skills in the highly competitive world of manga.

KANAKO lives and works out of her studio in London. She managed and directed the project as well as colouring and rendering the artwork digitally using her wealth of knowledge in graphic design.

www.manga-media.com
www.thorogood.net

Collect all the Alex Rider books

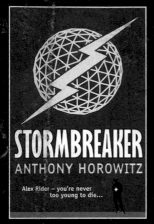
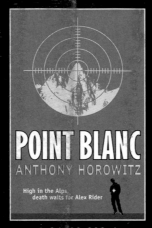
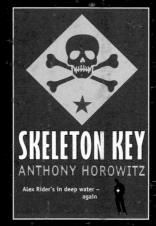
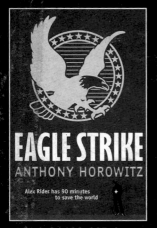

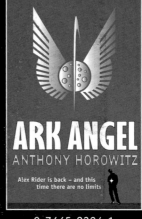
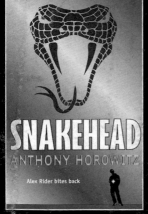